MW01174432

DAWN
is *Joyful*

Trudy & Martin
and family

I hope you enjoy my book.
God bless!

[signature]

Marlene Dawn Melnychuk

DAWN IS JOYFUL

Copyright © 2012 by Marlene Dawn Melnychuk

Unless otherwise indicated, all scriptures taken from the Holy Bible, New International Version®, NIV®. Copyright © 1973, 1978, 1984, 2011 by Biblica, Inc.™ Used by permission of Zondervan. All rights reserved worldwide. Scripture quotations marked (NLT) are taken from the Holy Bible, New Living Translation, copyright © 1996, 2004, 2007 by Tyndale House Foundation. Used by permission of Tyndale House Publishers, Inc., Carol Stream, Illinois 60188. All rights reserved.

ISBN:978-1-77069-466-8

Word Alive Press
131 Cordite Road, Winnipeg, MB R3W 1S1
www.wordalivepress.ca

WORD ALIVE PRESS
Just Write!

Library and Archives Canada Cataloguing in Publication
Melnychuk, Marlene Dawn, 1958-
    Dawn is joyful ; an autobiography / Marlene Dawn Melnychuk.
ISBN 978-1-77069-466-8

    1. Melnychuk, Marlene Dawn, 1958-. 2. Encephalitis--Patients--Biography. 3. Cerebral palsied--Biography. 4. Women with disabilities--Biography. I. Title.
RC390.M45 2012   362.196'8320092   C2012-901248-3

Trust in the Lord with all your heart,
and lean not on your own understanding;
in all your ways acknowledge Him,
and He shall direct your paths.
(Proverbs 3:5–6, NKJV)

This book is dedicated to my mom and dad,
and to my Uncle Joe Kozak,
who had cerebral palsy and was a kindred spirit.

contents

introduction

This book is dedicated to those who have allowed me to share this wonderful story of answered prayer in my life. It would be a privilege for me to know each one of you.

It would be amazing to share firsthand such a remarkable testimony of God's love and faithfulness in my life. I'm delighted to be granted this opportunity to share my life story with all of you. Thank you for opening your heart to me. My prayers have been to become more courageous and have an attitude that God would be pleased with as I share my experiences.

I wish to be a self-advocate for people who have encephalitis as their disability. I hope to be an example of strength as well as an encourager. I can give people with encephalitis a voice and educate people about more than just the medical element of this disease.

For someone with encephalitis, or something like it, it is hard, very hard, to succeed the first time you try something, but, as I have learned, it doesn't help to be frustrated if you fail. Try again and keep trying. Never put yourself down.

I hope this story inspires and enlightens you.

acknowledgements

There are many people in my life I am very thankful for and wish to acknowledge, especially my family and friends who encouraged me in becoming all that I am today.

I am very proud to be a grand-pk (pastor's kid), as my paternal grandparents were in the ministry. My paternal grandmother was a great woman of prayer also. Both sets of grandparents were very supportive of me.

Mom and Dad met each other in an old country school when they were in Grade One and they were inseparable from that time on. God gave my parents the second twinkle in their eye when I was born two years after my older sister, Wendi.

They were, and are, very compassionate parents and I feel very special to be their daughter. I'm thankful to God that they are my parents.

My sister Wendi is a very protective and joyful big sister who liked to play a lot of pranks on me when we were growing up, some which I have shared in my story. She married George, who quickly became my equally protective big brother.

They gave me two wonderful nephews, Taryn and Josh, who are very special to me. I love to tickle and joke around with them, giving them a lot of love. They are very bright boys who have married exceptional women—Lyndsay and Jen, respectively.

Marlene Dawn Melnychuk

So many people have made a special difference in my life, and although I cannot name you all here I wish to thank you very much.

letters

From Friends and Physicians

It is an honour for me to share a few words about Marlene Melnychuk. Our association goes back to the time when I served as Pastor of Central Tabernacle in Edmonton, Alberta, 1969–1978.

Marlene's smile, excitement, and warm personality is what I remember most about her. While we all face challenges, Marlene has faced much greater challenges, yet there has been an underlying quality which has caused her to rise above them. Much credit goes to her parents, John and Lydia, who deeply love her and in her young years led her in the direction of the Lord Jesus Christ and His Church. Her sister Wendy has also been of great support. When I look at Marlene, I see the joy and love of her Lord reflected in her countenance.

Marlene Dawn Melnychuk

The years have passed, but the picture in my mind of Marlene is one I cherish. My prayer is that the days ahead will continue to bring the joy, strength, and peace which comes from our Lord.

—Pastor George C. Smith

There are people who come into our lives and quickly pass. Others, like the Melnychuks, come and stay. They leave a lasting legacy, a legacy that has a lifelong benefit and eternal value.

I first met the Melnychuk family in the 1970s at Central Tabernacle in Edmonton—John and Lydia and those two wonderful sisters, Wendy and Marlene. They were committed and faithful people, generous in love.

I have always considered Marlene a special friend. We have enjoyed a spiritual bond in Christ. The truth of Michael W. Smith's song rings true in that friendship—"Friends are friends forever when the Lord is Lord of them." Proverbs 18:24 echoes this same truth: *"A man of many companions may come to ruin, but there is a friend who sticks closer than a brother."* Thank you, Marlene, for that special friendship.

Marlene has a contagious and winning smile! She has brought real joy to so many people. Our memories of her are many and rich. They reach back to children's and youth ministry days at Central—the friends, the events, the services, and so many special times. Marlene was there and one with us.

I relish many things about Marlene, but the best gift she could ever give us was and is the gift of her spirit. And so, I pay tribute to my special friend. God bless you.

—Pastor Gerry Johnson

This letter relates to Marlene Melnychuk's situation. The patient has been diagnosed as having choreoathetosis. This essentially causes her to have repeated motions, particularly on the left side of her body. These increase when she is stressed. Despite the disorder, which really has been a lifelong challenge, Marlene has valiantly coped with her condition. In fact, for many years she was actively employed.

She has always shown courage and has attempted to maintain herself quite mobile despite her condition. Even now, she is very reluctant to utilize aids such as a wheelchair or scooter too much, as she worries that she will lose the ability to walk. We have tried various medications for her difficulties over the years, and none have worked very well for her, unfortunately.

She has had a number of setbacks secondary to her condition, including a fall which resulted in a head injury, but, yet again, she has rebounded. One of the most amazing aspects of her situation has always been her positive attitude, which I suspect has been an encouragement to others. She really embodies the goal of the Glenrose, that being to allow patients to function despite their disabilities. I have been most impressed by Marlene's desire to maintain her cheerfulness despite her challenges. I feel that we, as a society, have a tendency to complain easily when faced by challenges much less daunting than Marlene's and her attitude should be an example to all of us.

One of the difficulties not unique to Marlene but to patients with various disabilities is the fact that other individuals, be they health care professionals or family, often make decisions for the patient which may decrease their independence. I believe at times that Marlene chafes and finds that others, because of their worry, place her under an "umbrella."

We as health care professionals often see a similar response in well-meaning family members. My epilepsy patients are another example where families are so worried that the patients will have seizures that they do not allow them independence. Obviously, safety is critically important in the care of our patients, but on the other hand it is also important to try to maintain them as independent as their circumstances allow.

—*Ken G. Makus*
M.D., FRCP(C) Neurology

Marlene Melnychuck began her career at the Glenrose Rehabilitation Hospital in 1983 and worked as an aide in Pediatrics, the Adult Stroke Program, and Porter Services. Marlene's infectious laugh, her kind nature, and love for her patients and colleagues made every day a special day for everyone at the Glenrose Hospital who came in contact with her.

In 2005, Marlene retired from the Glenrose after twenty-four years of service. The book you now hold in your hands is the culmination of her life experiences as a person living with encephalitis, and her determination to be the best she can be. Congratulations, Marlene, on your accomplishments.

—*Isabel Henderson*
Senior Operating Officer
Glenrose Rehabilitation Hospital

I am a clinical psychologist at the Glenrose Rehabilitation Hospital in Edmonton, a job I have enjoyed holding over the past twenty-five years. I remember over the years seeing Marlene at work in the Glenrose, sometimes pushing big stacks of supplies and equipment, and always with a ready smile and greeting as she went by. She always had a kind and friendly greeting for staff and patients alike.

Then I got to know Marlene in a different way after she was gravely injured in a fall down some stairs. She suffered a significant brain injury and, when I met her through our follow-up clinic, was in the midst of once again working to build back her life and regain the independence which had always been so important to her—such an irony for her in that she had spent good parts of her childhood obtaining therapy at the Glenrose before becoming a proud staff member. Now, once again as an adult, she was back in the role of being a patient at the Glenrose.

Despite the seriousness of her fall, Marlene was soon on the comeback trail and exuded the positive attitude, humour, and refusal to give up that I soon gathered had been lifelong traits. Her determination to regain her independence was unstoppable and she showed the spunk and drive that I suspect marked her early years of learning to deal with physical challenges after her diagnosis of encephalitis. Despite what I think must have been painful and difficult life events, Marlene always was able to focus on the positive side of life and often attributed this to her faith in a higher power and the love and support she had from family and friends. She has been amazing in her recovery from the brain injury and once again "beat the odds" in what she was able to achieve.

I am so very pleased to see Marlene fulfill her dream of writing a book about her life, which I think can give a sense of hope and inspire others to never give up, no matter what life hands us.

—*Jean McLeod*
Registered Psychologist

My family knows there's somewhere where we'll always belong, a place where we can laugh, love, and share joyful thoughts in life... where we have hugs and lots of support from those who cares for us in difficult times.

Families share everyday moments and wonderful memories. Even when we're apart, we share a closeness that distance and time can't erase.

For our family is a place in everyone's heart.

—Unknown

one

Growing Up at My Family's Side

Before I begin the story about my life with encephalitis, I have to mention my childhood and my family, because without them, and their prayers and support, I would probably be a completely different person with a different story. They helped me overcome many struggles in my life and encouraged me in my goals and dreams.

There are four people in my immediate family: my father, my mother, my older sister Wendi, and myself. Outside my immediate family, I have a huge number of cousins, aunts, and uncles—almost too many to count. My mom's parents had fifteen children and my father came from a family of thirteen. Each of them got married and had children of their own, and so on and so on… so I really do have a huge family.

A major aspect of my family is the church and having a relationship with Jesus Christ. My grandfather on my father's side was a pastor and his wife, my grandmother, was a woman of faith, a prayer warrior for her family and community.

My grandfather was the first Ukrainian pastor in the Edmonton area. He built a church on 97th Street in Edmonton and had quite a number of people in his congregation. Many were recent Ukrainian immigrants who couldn't understand much of the English language.

The church was like a family and people helped out wherever they could. I've been told that when I was a newborn, I came to church in my mother's arms and someone from the congregation would take me in their arms all service so that my mom could have a rest.

When I was a little older, my sister Wendi and I would get in the back seat of our family car after church and my parents would ask us what the minister had spoken about that day. We usually wouldn't remember or wouldn't know. Today, I ask my mom and dad the same question to see if they remember.

One thing I just love about church is the singing. I have always loved to sing. My favourite song is "This Little Light of Mine." When I'm in a bad mood, I'll just break out into song.

The church and the message of Jesus Christ has given me a definite purpose in life and helped me to understand the reason for my trials. It has also been a place where people have been encouraging and helpful to me and my family during both our good and bad times.

The ministers I had when I began going to a different church from my parents were always interested in what I was accomplishing or involved in. When they were gone on holidays and came back, they would always make it a point to ask me how I was doing. It seems like God just has this thing with me.

Whenever I go out and meet new people, they don't forget me! It's nice to have people who are like that, people I can smile at and have a good conversation with.

Growing up in the church gave me such a sense of the love and faithfulness of God. When I go to church, God gives me a peace about everything and a smile and a voice.

My grandparents, my mother's parents, also lived near Edmonton. My grandfather was a farmer and my grandmother a homemaker. They were married in the Ukraine. My grandfather immigrated to Canada first, leaving my mother and their six children behind. My mother came a little later, but sadly she had to leave one of her children behind. My uncle Joe had cerebral palsy and had to be left in the Ukraine with his grandmother. My grandmother wrote to him all the time and missed him a lot, but couldn't visit him very often because of travelling costs.

My parents are such a great example of what parents should be. They are supportive and loving and have always kept our family strong. I couldn't have asked for a better fit for myself, and I love them dearly.

My dad is now retired but still keeps busy by transporting cars to and from different places for a company. My mom is an excellent housekeeper and mother. I was on her apron strings all the time, especially after my sickness.

My sister Wendi is a wonderful big sister. I know that it was probably difficult for her growing up with a sister who needed extra attention and care all the time, and I really appreciate her as my sister and friend.

Wendi found a fantastic husband named George. I was so excited when their sons were born and I became an aunt. First came Taryn, and then Josh. When they were little, I had a lot of fun shopping for Christmas presents for them. One year, I bought them some markers for the bathtub. Needless to say, Wendi wasn't too impressed with the mess they made, but that's the good thing about being an aunt—you can't really get into too much trouble, because everyone knows it's your job to get your nephews and nieces cool stuff.

The boys were, and still are, so much fun. When Taryn was three years old, my father put him on a riding lawnmower and he drove himself all around the barn. Everyone was a little nervous about him taking control of such a big machine at his age, but my dad said Taryn was a great driver and very smart. He trusted him. The only thing that happened was that he clipped the top of a tree root, but the lawnmower stayed on all four wheels.

My mom and dad were living on the farm when Taryn was born and the little toddler seemed to like all kinds of things about the ranch. One day, he was visiting his "baba" (Ukrainian for Grandma) and was outside on the concrete following a little insect. My mom saw him pick up the bug and pick it apart. He was a curious kid.

My sister and her husband moved to Fort McMurray for George's job, and that's where they had their second son. Josh was such a rambunctious child. They are both quite the characters.

Taryn and Josh have grown up to be incredible young men of whom I am unbelievably proud. They have chosen beautiful and outstanding young women to be their wives. They were both married the same year, a month apart from each other. Taryn is married to Lyndsay and Josh is married to Jen.

Presently, each couple works at the same place as their spouse, which to me seems really nice. Lyndsay and Taryn are at the University of Alberta. Lyndsay works for Campus Crusade as a team leader and Taryn is working on his doctorate in oil research. He once let me read a paper he was working on and some of those words were an inch and a half long! He was also helping his professor teach some of the classes before his doctorate, while he was doing his master's degree. Taryn once delivered a paper at a conference in Europe. He is quite the brain.

Jen is a registered nurse in a hospital in Calgary and Josh works as a security officer there. He is also a firefighter. He graduated with his business degree before he was married and realized that he didn't want to do that for the rest of his life, so he decided to become a firefighter and loves it.

My sister has always been a good tease. I think she has slowed down a bit, but she used to love scaring me and pulling pranks on me. I loved it, too, most of the time; she was really good at it. She would often make it her goal to surprise or to scare me when we were younger. She would turn off the lights and grab me, or wait until I came to the bottom of the stairs and then jump out at me.

One time, she scared me while I was in the bathtub. I was soaking in some nice warm water and she snuck into the washroom and flung an ice cold pitcher of water over the shower curtain. It splashed me right on my head, scaring the willies out of me. She loved to do things like that.

Another memory I have of Wendi while we were growing up was her sixteenth birthday. She had gotten her driver's license and our dad wanted her to take a drive around the block. I came with. Unfortunately, the car was a stick shift and we kept going back and forth and back and forth. I got whiplash. Eventually, after some practice, she got the hang of it and ended up driving that car really well.

Wendi is now working for Petro Canada in their Calgary office and George is a computer analyst for a big oil company.

I am close to many of my cousins, and they've been so supportive of me as well. I've been on a few trips with them and a few have helped me gather photos and remember stories for the writing of this book.

As I have mentioned, my family is a major part of my life and I could not have achieved what I have today without their help and answered prayers.

Drawing is a special gift that God has given Marlene.

For none of us lives to himself alone and none of us dies to himself alone. If we live, we live to the Lord; and if we die, we die to the Lord. So, whether we live or die, we belong to the Lord.
—Romans 14:7–8 (NKJV)

two

What Happened to Me

"There is a reason for Marlene."

These words, spoken by my mother, were words of faith during a difficult time. Having just heard from the doctors that her toddler daughter might not make it, she was driven her to her knees.

It is with this event that my story begins.

I was born on August 30, 1958. My parents tell me that, as a young child, I was very precocious. I learned to walk and talk early on and was always bold and independent. I loved animals and was happy when my mom and dad decided to move to a brand new area. I was one and a half years old and Wendi was three.

Our new home was just outside of Edmonton and our nextdoor neighbours were a young family of five. They had lived there for a long time and had a hobby farm. My sister and

I loved it because they had cows, dogs, chickens, cats, birds, and many other animals to keep us entertained.

I was in my element and quickly began to love their old and docile dog, Hubert. Hubert was really tame and let us climb up and jump on him. He easily put up with all of our roughhousing; he would even lick our faces as we played with him. But this uncharacteristic lethargy wasn't just due to Hubert being a tame and domestic dog.

Hubert was unwell and carried airborne ticks, which caused him to have a sleeping sickness. Because of this dog's sickness, my family's life changed dramatically just two days before I was to celebrate my second birthday.

Through that night and the next morning, I suffered a high fever. When my parents walked through the door, they could hear me moaning. The pressure on my brain was so severe. They took efforts to cool my fever with cold baths, but the baths were in vain. I was quickly taken to the emergency room at the Royal Alexandra Hospital near downtown Edmonton.

Tthe doctors first attributed the high fever to tonsillitis, which I had a history of. They gave me a shot of penicillin and sent us home. We didn't even make it home from the hospital when I fell into a coma. My parents immediately rushed me back to the hospital.

I spent almost three weeks in the hospital before a diagnosis was made. The doctors still weren't sure what the illness was, but they were leaning toward meningitis.

During these weeks, I was brought into an oxygen tent in Intensive Care. I slept on an ice pillow in an effort to bring down my fever, which at some times exceeded 105°F. The doctor told my parents that I was suffering from encephalitis. At the end of these three weeks, my fever finally broke. I spent another five weeks in a semi-coma. It didn't look good.

The doctors tried to prepare my parents for the worst. They informed them that I might not make it, and that if I did there was a great chance I could face serious mental and physical disabilities.

I should add here that there were other children who played with Hubert that were affected as well. Some of the other children from around our neighbourhood suffered in the same way and landed in the hospital as well. One little boy, in particular, had a very serious brain disorder and his older sister, who was my age, was diagnosed with encephalitis, the same as me. The older children, including Wendi, recovered well, likely because their age put them at an advantage for having more immunity.

Hubert himself passed away two weeks after the incidents.

> "All who have a really blessed life are filled with a lot of joy and happiness.
> God will put smiles on everyone's face."
> —Marlene Melnychuk

What Is Encephalitis?

Encephalitis is an inflammation of the brain that is caused by a virus. It's an uncommon disease and it affects about one in every two hundred thousand people, though it seems more likely to hit children, the elderly, and individuals with a weak immune system.

It can be caused by a herpes simplex virus that attacks the brain, but that is very rare. Encephalitis can also be caused by a rare complication of Lyme disease that is spread by airborne ticks, or rabies spread by animals. It can be spread by mosquitoes, too. Childhood diseases such as rubella, measles, chickenpox, rubella, and mumps also can cause a mild form of encephalitis. People with weakened immune systems can get it from certain parasites and bacterial infections.

For those who experience a mild form of encephalitis, symptoms include feeling sick, a fever, headaches, and loss of appetite and energy. A more severe form may include symptoms like a severe headache, vomiting, memory loss, confusion, coma, and difficulty speaking or hearing.

joyful

Marlene Dawn Melnychuk

"*When you have a rainbow deep down in your heart, your smile will shine bright and it will brighten everyone's day.*"
—Marlene Melnychuk

four

Recovering and Dealing with Disabilities

Twice during my lengthy recovery, I turned blue. My parents were called twice by the hospital and told that I might not make it. After one of these phone calls, my mother collapsed to her knees, frozen, and silently told herself, *There is a reason for Marlene.* Surely enough, when my parents arrived at the hospital, I had returned to a much normal colour. From here, it was a slow but steady adventure to recovery.

Recovery and accepting a new life is a difficult thing to do and I'm very fortunate to have a loving family and godly parents. My grandparents—as well as my aunts, uncles and cousins—were prayer warriors for me and my immediate family. My family's faith was strong as we all went through these times together. I'm glad they prayed for my life. Their prayers were definitely with me during my time of recovery. It was an exhausting time, but I was able to make progress.

Eight weeks passed since that fateful day when I fell into a coma. I had lost all coordination in my body. I couldn't sit, walk, or even speak. During this time I had a lot of visitors; family members, pastors, and friends of the family came to visit me. My mother was faithful, watching over me every day by my bedside. With instructions from the doctors, she watched eagerly for my responsiveness. I was so weak. I couldn't lift my head, but I was able to look around. I recognized my mother's walk whenever she came into the room from the hallway.

My mother spent time reciting nursery rhymes to me, and eventually she was able to tell that I was following along with her. As the days passed, I became better and stronger.

One day my mother came into the room like every other day, but on this day I was standing with my head above the crib rail, ready to greet her with my first words since I fell sick.

"Hi Mom."

To my mother, that was the day the heavens shone through.

Around the ninth week of recovering in the Royal Alexander Hospital, I was allowed to go back home. It wasn't all back to normal, however, and my parents had to keep a close watch on me all the time. My crib had to be within arm's reach of my parents at all times.

Life as we knew it had now changed forever.

The encephalitis left me with mental and physical disabilities. In particular, the left side of my body suffered severe tremors, rendering my left arm and leg completely useless. Everything I had learned before the age of two was gone. I had to relearn how to walk, how to speak, and how to carry out fine motor skills. This all had to be rediscovered with just one good arm and one good leg to work with.

Everyday activities that had once came easy to me were now a great challenge. My muscles had been weakened by my illness. Actions that were designed for two hands had to be learned using one hand, and the spasms on my left side added an extra hurdle to learning how to walk.

At the Glenrose

It was like being a newborn all over again. The first thing they taught me to do again was to chew and swallow. I worked with physiotherapists and occupational therapists to help me get close to where I had been before the illness.

Videotaping was one of the approaches used to help me learn to walk in my new condition. They taped my progress until I was eighteen. As an adult, I was able to get a hold of one of those tapes and watch myself. The video showed me as a child crying nonstop when they tried to get me to overcome the useless left leg so I could walk.

When I was older, about seven or eight, I remember dressing up in a large one-piece bathing suit for the videotaping session. I adorned the outfit with sunglasses and socks, then walked down the runway like a movie star.

This stage of my rehabilitation—the walking and talking—was learned at the Glenrose Rehabilitation Centre.

Next was the CP (cerebral palsy) clinic. Since my encephalitis had left me with similar symptoms to cerebral palsy sufferers, this was the destination for which I would wake up at 6:00 a.m. I began going there at the age of three and a half years and followed a strict schedule of physiotherapy, speech therapy, and occupational therapy. I had to take a nap during the day, too, but there wasn't a lot of time allotted for that activity. My exhaustion at the end of the day couldn't be described.

I found trouble during this time. I don't know what time of year it was—maybe in the fall or maybe in the spring—but I started to get really annoyed about going for a nap. I didn't want to sleep. One particular day, I had a beautiful barrette in my hair. The therapists laid me down for my nap, but I needed to use up my remaining energy. There was no way I was going to go to sleep this time.

I don't know why I did this, but I made my way over to an electrical outlet, sat down, and took the pretty barrette out of my blond hair. I stuck that barrette right into the socket and was, of course, electrocuted. The plastic part of the barrette melted and I think that's when my hair became curly.

The nurses noticed right away and rushed over to me. That's when I knew I was in trouble.

The nurses told me they were going to phone my mother and father. I was terrified. I begged them not to because I knew I would get a talking to at home. I was reprimanded at the clinic as well. They gave me a curfew and a major talk about how to behave during therapy.

But something good came out of all of this: I have curly hair. It's also one of my favourite stories to tell about my time at the Glenrose.

Before my illness, I had been able to walk normally. After the encephalitis, and upon entering the CP clinic, the doctors recommended a heel cord surgery in my foot which involved strengthening it, releasing it, and putting it back together again. I had to wear a long boot after this (this was before the advent of the use of plastics in medicine, so the boot was both uncomfortable and unattractive). When I continued to have trouble straightening my foot, I had yet another surgery to repair my club foot. I was around the age of five or six years old.

This physical issue made it difficult to buy regular shoes, and all I ever wanted—and have ever wanted—was a nice pair of fancy red shoes. The wish had been a strong one since the day my mother took me on our semi-annual shopping trip for shoes—practical ones, of course. We needed to find good, strong shoes with good grip that would be able to accommodate a brace. The brace needed to fit between the bottom of the shoe and the sole; the brace would then go up my leg to my knee, where it was strapped in place.

I was okay with getting these shoes, but my eye caught a pair of bright red impractical non-grip dress shoes for little girls. My heart leapt. I wanted those shoes so badly that I asked my mom for them. I knew it wasn't be a possibility, and I never got them, but I have remembered those gorgeous shoes from then until now. My mom remembered, too, and a couple of years ago she sneakily took a pair of my white running shoes and spray painted them a ruby red colour. I was really surprised!

I know that you cannot take material things with you into heaven, but someday, when I pass away, I hope to wear those red running shoes at my funeral.

The operation on my heel cord took place at the Royal Alexandra Hospital. All I really remember about the hospital is that it seemed old and dingy. After I was moved to the Glenrose, I was sick of operations and hospitals. I think I made it difficult for the nurses there. The nurses weren't mean, but I could tell their patience was short when dealing with me. It was hard to cope.

I had a lot of visits from family and friends. I remember the minister from our church coming to see me a lot while I was there. He would visit with me and bring a lot of encouragement. Another great aspect of him visiting was that at each visit he would bring chocolate. As the years progressed, the youth pastor came to visit with me as well. He would talk with me and try to lift me into a state in which I believed there was nothing wrong with me. In fact, God healed me so many times that it's impossible for me to comprehend just how many times it has happened.

I received speech therapy from an Englishwoman. Believe it or not, I ended up with a lovely English accent for some time after this. I also attended school while I was at the Glenrose, a sort of pre-kindergarten.

I was in therapy for a long time—about three weeks. The room I was in was huge and had ten cubicles, one of which I was in. A wall with smoked glass provided some privacy. When I was finally walking and finished therapy, I had no remorse leaving. The day I was to leave, I got up, walked to the door, and said to the nurses, "So long, farewell. If I ever see you again, I hope it's not in this room."

I did see that room and the cubicles again, about two years later when I was seven. I had to get a second heel cord surgery, but this time it was more fun.

After the surgery, I had a huge cast going up my leg to my thigh, and after a week or so they lowered the cast, so it only came up to my knee.

One time I was in the physical therapy department and needed to go back to my room, which was on the other side of the Glenrose. I wasn't patient enough to wait for one of the porters to come and wheel me back, and I knew how to get there, so I figured I could do it all by myself.

There was a ramp on my way and I didn't think it looked too steep. I had my right arm and leg free—the good side—and I figured I could hold on to the wheel and steady my chair while I went down the ramp. I easily made it down without a problem.

Then I turned the corner quickly, and went down another ramp with a big incline. At the end of that one was a brick wall. Whipping down the ramp and missing the brick wall at the end was exhilarating. After all that excitement, I didn't know where I was anymore until I saw some nurses from my unit eating in the cafeteria. I couldn't find a way to get back up the ramp where I was supposed to be without the nurses noticing me.

When they saw me, they ran over.

"Marlene! How did you get down the ramp? What are you doing here?" said one of them.

Oh no, I thought. *Here comes another lecture.*

Indeed, the nurses told me they were going to have to tell my parents what had happened. Again, I pleaded with them not to call up my mother and father—and also my doctor. But I guess they had to and I sat through some more lectures on being careful with myself. I felt guilty, but it had felt really good going down those ramps. I loved being a daredevil.

I took part in my share of dangerous stunts growing up. Sometimes they ended badly, but it was a fun way of dealing with my situation. If you're willing to try something fun, try it and see how far it gets you. But if you smack into the wall, that's no good. If you don't, you feel on top of the world.

Many memories were created and stories weaved at the old Glenrose building. After extensive physiotherapy and speech therapy, I was so grateful for finally regaining my ability to walk and talk.

[I am] confident of this very thing, that He who has begun a good work in you will complete it until the day of Jesus Christ.
—Philippians 1:6 (NKJV)

five

Outside the Glenrose Hospital

Rehabilitation after my club foot surgery took a few fulltime months in the Glenrose. Following this, I was allowed home. I was certainly my mother's child during this time; I was strung to her apron. She couldn't leave my sight, not even to take the garbage out.

I started public school at the age of six.

I took special classes from a school in the neighbourhood and took great pride in becoming the teacher's pet. One teacher took a particular interest in me. She thought I could do everything and anything and gave me the privilege of performing special tasks in class. I once took ill while in her class. She stopped by to see me at home and left a gift: her cat. She was the sweetest teacher I ever had.

Marlene Dawn Melnychuk

When I was out of public school, in Grade Three, my brain swelled and attacked my memory, causing me to learn at a slower pace. This was okay, though, because it gave me time to learn slowly and do things quickly.

In Grade Four, I entered L.Y. Carins Vocational School. Luckily enough, I am a bus person, and reaching this school required a great amount of travel. I enjoyed my time here tremendously, and I remember with great fondness the art/drama teacher who passed on to me an appreciation for both of these subject areas. This teacher, who encouraged me and helped me to love art, was the greatest thing since sliced bread. I still do artwork to this day.

In a production put on by the drama team, I played the part of a puppeteering professor. It was the largest acting part—the lead. As all good puppeteers do, I made the students under my control dance and play. I certainly looked the part of an unkempt professor when I dressed up and messed up my hair. I did everything to the last detail. It was so much fun.

Another of my greatest accomplishments during my vocational school career came through the teachings of my art/drama teacher. The school hosted a contest encouraging students to submit drawings. The winning entry would become the school's logo. I took a piece of my own identity—Ukrainian art—and personalized it further. I couldn't believe it when I learned I had won the contest. That piece is still the school's logo. I'm pleased that this little piece of me will go down in history as the vocational school's logo, a symbol of what other students there can accomplish. To add to my feelings of pride, I also received a cheque for twenty-five dollars.

The school also taught me math, science, and reading. I also took a baking class. I really like to bake, but will admit it's a little difficult to do with only one good hand. I took sewing, drama, and art—but my favourite class, hands down, was art class.

Sewing class proved to be a challenge, but I did come out of it with a finished product. It took me a year to make a jumpsuit for that class, and I had a lot of help cutting the material. My mom helped me out when I was in trouble and I was able to get it done in time for a fashion show held at the school.

Later on, I ran for class president. It was a little nerve-wracking when I had to speak in front of the class, and then the whole school, but I won. I remember being so excited to be the class president. I was hopping up and down and in a really good mood.

A lot of responsibilities came with being class president and I had fun organizing and planning. We voted on activities, held some dances, and brought people outside of the school to speak to our class on different topics.

Even though I did well in vocational school, and enjoyed my time there, I couldn't avoid the bullying.

Some of the kids could be really cruel and immature with their words. It hurt. They didn't understand my situation and sometimes targeted me with teasing. Sometimes I would go home and cry, unable to believe why so many kids were heartless when it came to others who had disabilities.

My mother was there for me during this time. One time when I came home crying, she had some beautiful words for me, words that I haven't forgotten: "Marlene, everybody has a disability. People can physically see yours, but a lot of people have disabilities that you cannot see."

Beautiful words from my beautiful mother.

The teasing stopped after a while when I met a really big girl who acted as my guardian and helped protect me. She was in my class and had brown hair and brown eyes. I think she saw the teasing and had enough compassion for me to help make it stop.

"If you touch her, I'll touch you," she would say to the bullies.

People got the message and started to leave me alone completely.

Near the end of my time at vocational school, I did two work placement programs. I loved both of them.

The first was at the Glenrose Rehabilitation Centre, a place with which I was already familiar. During my rehabilitation, I had attended an early kindergarten class. This time, I got to experience what it was like to help out the teacher wherever I could. I admired her; these children had somebody to look up to... somebody I could look up to. This experience reaffirmed my love for children, as I mentored one of the pranksters in some old tricks. The student caught on quickly and was soon coming up with his own ideas for practical jokes. It was good for me to revisit my childhood. I could relate to these children—their struggles and their joys, their happiness and frustrations, their weaknesses and strengths.

If the kids were paying attention, I shared about all the things I could do despite my disability, and what they could therefore accomplish as well. I could completely relate to these children because I had been in the same situation when I was their age.

I worked with one boy who was there because he had almost drowned in the pool in his family's backyard. I sensed that he needed a little more of a helping hand, so I gave him some extra attention. We became really good friends. I became like his older sister and could guide him and get him to try new things. If he could do them, it was great, but if he couldn't do them on the first try, I would tell him not to put himself down.

After all, it was great that he had at least tried to do it. I would encourage him to try it again, or I would assist him myself.

He would come and see me every morning. It was wonderful for me to see how he grew and how much I was able to help him.

There were also children there who had no mobility or ways to communicate. They would just lie there. I'd take time to sing to them, talk to them, hold their hand, and just be there to tell them that they weren't alone. There were other children who were very dismayed about having to stay there. I did my best to make them feel comfortable. I would tell them that they would be very happy when they were able to learn and do things again.

Working with the children at the Glenrose Rehabilitation Centre was great. It gave me an opportunity to encourage others. This was such a valuable time of my life. Today, when I'm out in public, sometimes I come across kids who I used to work with. They'll recognize me, come right up to me, and talk.

My second work placement program landed me a daycare job on Whyte Avenue. There were approximately twenty-five children at the daycare from the ages of zero to five. I loved this placement as well. The children would be curious about my disability and ask me why I was different. I didn't mind those questions at all, because I liked talking about what I have and the children accepted me.

During these summer months, I played with the children inside the home and out. We also went for walks and I read to them. My love for children—for working, playing, and interacting with them—became even clearer to me at this point. This job taught me a lot about myself and others.

Other than the teasing, I felt like I really fit in at vocational school and I thoroughly enjoyed the programs and my time there. The positive feedback I received and their excellent curriculum made me feel prepared and excited to enter the world when I graduated at age eighteen.

University of Alberta

When I was in Grade Twelve, I began to take an art class at the University of Alberta. My brother-in-law, George, was a student there at the time and had found out about this course. He suggested that I try it out and see if I liked it. He had a class going on at the same time as the art class, so we drove there together. It was one evening a week and I really enjoyed the class. I still love to draw and have a couple of works in a sketchbook.

We learned the basics of drawing and I soon got the hang of it. We started out learning how to draw fruit, and then we moved on to flowers. Drawing still life came easily to me, but when it came to painting... well, that was difficult for me. I had drawn some poinsettias on a canvas and thought, *This looks pretty good. Maybe I should try to paint it.* I did just that, and I have to say that it looked terrible when I was finished. Maybe I'll try and painting again someday. I might learn from my mistakes and do better after some practice.

The other difficult part of the art class was when we studiedthe human body. It was a little awkward when the models came into the class and struck a pose. It was complicated for me to draw the human body.

The art class was very beneficial to me and it made me think more about what I could and couldn't do. It gave me confidence to try new things in life. I didn't get frustrated when I couldn't do something because there were a lot of things that I could do.

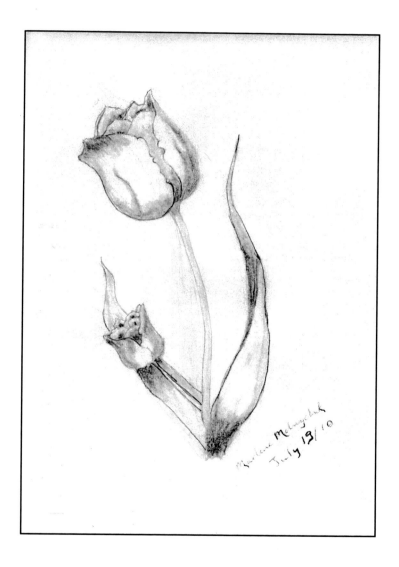

Marlene Dawn Melnychuk

I thank my God every time I remember you.
In all my prayers for all of you, I always pray with joy.
  —Philippians 1:3–4

six

Childhood and Fun Young Adult Stories

Marshmallows

This is one of my earlier memories, from when I was six years old. My mom and dad had gone somewhere for a little while—whether they went for a walk or were working in the garden, I don't recall. What I do remember is that they left me at home unsupervised for a short time.

To this day, I have quite a big sweet tooth. When I crave something sweet, there's no turning back. On this day, I searched the cupboards for something sugary and found a big bag of marshmallows. Well, that was it; those marshmallows didn't see what was coming to them. I wolfed down those sweet airy treats until the whole bag was gone. I didn't think it was a bad idea until my stomach started rumbling. Well, my stomach got angrier and angrier until I had to get that anger out.

Marlene Dawn Melnychuk

When my parents came back, they found me sick in the washroom. I reluctantly told them what had happened, and, like most parents, they just cautioned me to stay away from eating so much at a time. They had nothing to worry about because I didn't touch another marshmallow until I was nineteen years old.

Recreation

When I was young, I was kind of a loner, content to play all by myself. I was a little shy about meeting other kids my age. My sister saw this in me and made sure that I got away from that and became more adventurous and outgoing.

Wendi helped me get involved with activities that didn't involve clinging to my mom and dad. She would take me outside and let me run around with her and her friends. She once gave me a boost to get up on top of our backyard fence and in the wintertime she encouraged me to try skating. I was excited. I had been watching figure skating on television for a long time. To my young and naïve perspective, skating looked really easy. I was certain I would be able to do what the professionals did on television.

Skating definitely proved to be a challenge. My parents brought Wendi and me to the ice arena. I tried on some skates and got out on the ice, but of course my left foot wouldn't cooperate. My foot was supposed to be upright, but instead it kept moving around. My dad had to hold me up the whole time and I realized just how difficult it actually was. Skating, to say the least, wasn't working out. My dad tried to find a skate that had two blades on it instead of just one in the middle, but we didn't have any luck finding one.

Wendi would also take me sledding. We'd scream down the hill and it felt like I was travelling at rocket speeds. These are the childhood memories that I really treasure.

Horseback Riding

I love to try things that seem like they might be a challenge. If I can do it, great; if I can't, I'll try something else. One of the things I wanted to try was horseback riding. Our youth group from church went to a ranch outside of the city, and when we arrived there I could see these beautiful horses on top of a hill. The ranch itself was so picturesque.

I was excited to take on one of those horses. *What's the big deal about me getting on a horse?* I thought. *It looks easy. I can do it.*

The people I was with encouraged me to try, so my confidence steadily grew. We had to walk up the hill to get to the horses, which for me seemed like a very long walk. I was tired by the time we arrived

When I saw the horses, my excitement and anxiety about riding one of them escalated. These horses were huge when I saw them up close; nonetheless, I still wanted to challenge myself. I wanted to know if I could do it.

My friends and the people at the ranch were saying, "Oh, don't worry, Marlene. This horse is really tame. You'll love him."

So they hoisted me on this tall horse's back and somehow this horse just decided to take off—with me on him! I was too shocked to scream, so I held on for dear life while the horse ran through the pasture.

I slipped off to the side a few times during this fast-paced event, but fortunately was able to pull myself back into the right position. My only focus was to try to stay on the horse. A group of people were chasing after me, trying to make the horse slow down and save me from destruction, but they were too far behind to do any good.

This horse and I were quickly headed towards the trees.

This is it, I thought. *I can't hold on anymore.*

Sure enough, I went down and hit the soft earth. I wasn't hurt, but I could see the hooves of the horse coming toward my head and I felt the wind from them as they whipped by my face.

When I got up, the rancher was next to me.

"Well, Marlene, you'll have to try it again. Get back on that horse."

"No thanks," I said. "I'll just walk back."

The rancher understood and led me the whole way back. I didn't want to tell my parents, because I was okay and didn't want them to worry. I knew, though, that the story would get out amongst the parents of the young people in our youth group and that they would hear about it anyway. I gave them a phone call and told them what had happened.

I'm really glad I had this experience. Even with this disability, I could say that I had tried to learn to ride a horse. I had survived the experience. I loved the excitement.

Skiing

Our youth group also did winter events. One time, we all went skiing at Rabbit Hill in Edmonton. I had never done this before and, with the encouragement of my peers and my own ambition, I was fitted for a pair of skis.

They gave me a ski instructor who was very large and I took off to the bunny hill with him. Before I was allowed down the hill, the instructor had to go over a few skiing techniques. One of the things I remember is making the shape of a slice of pie with your skis to make yourself stop. I tried this, but my left leg wouldn't cooperate. I couldn't make a pie; instead, it looked more like a shaking, shivering "X."

I tried to ski anyway. I spent the whole evening falling after a couple of feet of gliding, then sliding down the rest of the hill on my behind. I didn't care at all that I fell so much. I had never attempted this before, and even though I wasn't a natural, I was having so much fun just trying.

The next day, I didn't have an easy time getting out of bed. I knew my parents were already up and enjoying the day; I also knew that if I wasn't up soon, my mom and dad would wonder what was wrong with me. I didn't want that to happen. I needed to avoid their questions.

I painfully and slowly unhinged my bones, loosened up my muscles, and finally sat up in bed. Sure, I was sore, but I wouldn't have missed the opportunity to ski. I was so happy that I'd tried it.

White Water Rafting

One of the most thrilling adventures I've had the privilege of trying is white water rafting. My cousin Willis invited me to go with the young people from church and I couldn't say no. I was nervous that Mom and Dad wouldn't let me go, so I didn't tell them what I was going to do.

We travelled out to Golden, British Columbia. We had to sign a waiver before we were allowed to get into the rafts. The rapids were huge; I remember that they were classified as "4.5." We all fit into three or four rafts, then took off down the threatening river.

We were tossed around all over the raft, but surprisingly no one in our group fell out. I wasn't scared at all. I enjoyed every rapid. I had it easy, though, because I was allowed to sit in the middle of the raft like a queen, and I didn't have to paddle at all.

There were times between rapids where the water was calm. We used this time to jump off the rafts and try to soak our friends in the other rafts.

All in all, it was a lot of fun. When I got home, though, I had to tell my parents what we had done on our trip to British Columbia. I had to really work on their forgiveness and it took me awhile to earn their trust back. I knew that I should have told them before I went. I made sure to leave Willis out of it, but he later took responsibility when he talked with my parents.

I would go again, given the chance. Camping and flying over the rapids was so much fun and I'm so happy to have this memory.

The Singing Christmas Tree

Every year in Edmonton, at Christmas time, there's an event called The Singing Christmas Tree where people from different churches get together to sing Christmas songs in a church. The organizers position the singers in a shape that resembles a Christmas tree. I've been part of the singing tree a couple of times, as well as some of my family members, and it's really quite something to be involved with.

One year, at a rehearsal, I ventured down the stairs from the stage. When I went down the first step, my left foot didn't cooperate and caught on the carpet. I slammed face first into the church's stucco wall. I hit my eye and ear, resulting in a lost pearl earring that I had bought from my trip to Hawaii.

My cousin Willis came running right away and took me and my bleeding head to the car. The car was his younger brother Peter's, so before I got in, Willis said, "Marlene, be careful not to get blood on the seats! I have to keep it clean!"

Willis drove me to the emergency room and let me off inside. He insisted on parking the car and waiting with me in the hospital. I didn't think it was necessary, because my apartment was right across from the hospital at the time and I could have easily crossed the street to get home. I guess he wanted to make sure I didn't faint or anything like that.

When I saw the doctor, Willis came with me. The doctor was young and good looking and I was treated well. I needed stitches. While the doctor put the stitches in, Willis began talking with the doctor about fishing. That's all I heard about the whole time he was putting stitches in me.

Willis asked if he could help me control the tremors in my arm by putting pressure on it during the procedure. After a while I felt a little dizzy, like I couldn't breathe, and the cloth on my face was beginning to get hot. Willis and the doctor kept talking, but fortunately the doctor noticed that I was pretty quiet and not looking so great. When he asked if I was okay, I asked Willis to ease up the pressure on my arm. After that, I was fine.

We were in there for about an hour and a half, all the while talking about fishing. I had about fifteen stitches because of that fall, but they healed up really well. The wound is pretty much invisible today.

Willis walked me home from the hospital. He was concerned about me staying the night in my apartment all by myself, but I finally convinced him that I would be fine.

Two weeks later, the doctor removed the stitches. Mom and Dad were a little worried about me when they heard the story, but they weren't too bad.

The good part about the story is that I got my pearl earring back. My cousin, who worked at the church, searched for it and found it.

Camping Adventure

When the chance came up to go on a church camping retreat in Radium, British Columbia, a girlfriend of mine and

I couldn't say no. The trip sounded great and I was excited to go and rough it in the great outdoors. We borrowed another girlfriend's tent and drove the miles together on the August long weekend.

We arrived early Saturday morning, set up our tent, ate our supper, and enjoyed the beautiful scenery. It was nice hot day. Later on in the evening, we decided to go to the Radium Hot Springs. It was. We soaked ourselves in the relaxing water and let our muscles marinate in the minerals.

Everything was going so well—until it began to rain. At first it was just a little sprinkle, but soon it began to pour. Sheets and sheets of rain plummeted down from the sky.

We hurried back to our tent, where my friend opened the zipper, went in, and then quickly came back out—drenched. There was about half a foot of water in the bottom of our tent. The pillows were floating and our sleeping bags were beyond saving.

Now the problem was, where were we going to sleep? My girlfriend soon came up with the idea that we sleep in her new car.

We left everything in the tent and split one blanket between the two of us. The rain continued to pour down and neither of us could sleep with the raindrops beating against the roof of the car all night.

The next day, we decided to drive to Banff. It was a funny morning, though, because we had such a tough time getting the water out of the tent. When we took it down, the water poured out like a river.

I was so tired. I slept all the way to Banff. It was definitely a trip to remember.

Marlene's parents on their wedding day.

Marlene and her sister, Wendi—the two twinkles in their parents' eyes.

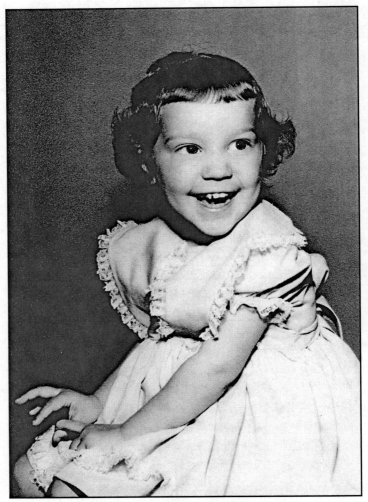

Marlene as a child, before she became sick.

*Marlene after she became sick—in a basket
with her very special teddy bear.*

A favourite hobby, playing and singing music.

Marlene, Wendi and their parents.

The whole family.

A white water rafting trip in Golden, BC.

A very special time parasailing on the island of Maui.

Marlene Dawn Melnychuk

> *But let all who take refuge in you be glad; let them ever sing for joy.*
>
> *Spread your protection over them, that those who love your name may rejoice in you.*
> —Psalm 5:11

seven

Life After School

When I was out of school, I lived with my parents for a while. Then they moved to a farm and I moved in to an apartment with my sister, Wendi. We had a really good time living together, but we didn't have too much money. I remember we didn't eat very much. When we would go home to visit Mom and Dad, they would order pizza and give us care packages to take back to our apartment. It was a really nice time in life.

Eventually, I moved out of the apartment and back into my parents' house. They lived on an eighty-acre piece of land with a nice wooded area.

One time, during the winter, Mom and Dad bought me a pair of snowshoes and I decided to go outside and try them out. There was a lot of snow on the ground. I started trekking through the snow toward the wooded area. When I finally got there, I fell and thought it was time to go back to the house. It was forty acres away, but I did it. It wasn't too cold, fortunately, because I had a snowsuit and other winter equipment on.

While I lived with my parents, I had a dog named Sam. Sam was a black and white German Shepherd and Collie cross... and very playful. I loved having him around and we played together a lot. He was really good at keeping me company when Mom and Dad weren't home. I played a lot of Frisbee with him.

One time, a man came to our farm whose name was also Sam. Sam, the dog, was jumping on Sam the man and we said, "Sam, get down!" Both Sam the dog and Sam the man got down when we gave the order.

When I went to Japan on a holiday, Sam's back legs gave out and it was necessary to put him down. My parents put him down while I was away, knowing it would have been difficult for me to go through. When I came back, my brother-in-law broke the news to me. I cried when he told me, but I do have some great memories of Sam.

Around this time, a man who lived in a nearby town needed a nanny and housekeeper for his home. He had three sons, the youngest of which was still home. I cleaned the house and was a babysitter to this young boy. It was a great job and I really appreciated the time and effort the dad put in for me to have this job. I worked there for about a year.

I eventually left my parents' home again after being invited to live with Loretta and Lana in an apartment in Edmonton. We had a lot of fun together and played pranks on each other, too. One time, my cousin Loretta was studying for school and looking for someplace quiet to do so. She went into a storage room, kind of like a big closet, and set up there. While she was in there, I put a chair under the doorknob and went to the living room to watch a hockey game.

I ended up falling asleep. When she tried to get out of the room and found the door locked, she called for someone to let her out. Nobody answered and she began to get irritated. She was pretty mad at me when I woke up. It wasn't funny then, but it is now.

It wasn't luxury, but I enjoyed living with them. There was only one bedroom, but we didn't care. Loretta was taking a computer course at NAIT and my other cousin, Pam, was going to Bible college and had a job at the post office. The quarters were a bit cramped, but we survived. We got along really well. They were like my little sisters.

Laugh when you can, apologize when you should, and let go of what you can't change. Play hard, forgive quickly, take changes, give everything, and have no regrets. Life's too short to be anything... but happy.

—Unknown

eight

Working at the Glenrose Hospital

oving back into the city, I decided to see if there was a volunteer position available at the Glenrose. After volunteering there for six months, they created a position for me to work with the kids. I was twenty-one at the time.

This position turned into a paid job when the nursing staff said they needed someone in the children's playroom fulltime. I'm not sure if it was management's decision or if the nurses spoke with some of the doctors for me to get this job, but it was very nice of them to do that.

My job allowed me to play with all kinds of kids facing different challenges. The patients ranged in age from infants to eighteen-year-olds. Some had cerebral palsy; others were there because of head injuries. I liked to tell them how to do things and get them in a good mood and excited for therapy. I liked to make them laugh.

Others were severely challenged and couldn't talk. The way they communicated was through blinking their eyes. For example, one blink meant no and two fast blinks meant yes.

There was one girl there in particular who I remember. I would keep her company and talk with her. She communicated by looking up for "yes" and down for "no."

I learned a lot working with these kids. I learned how to relate to them and about the difficult times they'd faced at such a young age. I tried my best to give them encouragement and moral support. I wanted to keep them from thinking bad thoughts about what could potentially happen in their lives.

"If you're trying to do something and you can't, never put yourself down," I remember saying to them. "If you try it again and again and you eventually get it, that's great! But if not, you can try something else and maybe you will succeed at that. Try and do something that you can do. Try everything that you want to do. Never think about putting yourself down."

I loved to get that message across. I wanted to show people that if their spirits were really were low about not doing something, there were other things they could achieve—big or small. It's not good to sit around and mope about not doing things; you should always try something new.

On occasion, it was really sad and heart-breaking to see the families these kids were a part of. A few of the families found it really difficult to deal with their child's new life and didn't feel qualified to handle them at their own house. Some of these children therefore went into other homes and care centres. That was really hard for me to see, because my family had been so supportive and wonderful. It really opened my eyes. I am very grateful to God for the life I've had.

Sometimes the children would bring tears to my eyes when they'd ask me to please stay when it was time for me to go home. They gave me a lot of joy. I, myself, am a person who learned to try things. If God gives me the strength to do something, then I'm going to do it.

This job was a dream come true. I used to pray about having a job at the Glenrose when I was little and taking therapy there. I was so happy that they decided to hire me. Sometimes I would think that people wouldn't understand why a rehabilitation centre would hire a handicapped woman, but I worked really hard there and loved my job.

During this time, I had been living with my cousins for about ten months. Pam lived closer to the Glenrose Rehabilitation Centre, in the nursing residence. She invited me to room with her and I tried that for about a year and a half. It was really handy getting to the Glenrose and I had a lot of fun living with her. The only thing that was challenging was that the washroom was at the end of the hallway outside our apartment and you had to run down the hall really quickly if you had to make use of it.

After a year and a half, I moved again. This time I got a bachelor apartment all by myself. It was at the HYS Centre near the Glenrose. It was a reasonable price so I grabbed the apartment right away.

My parents didn't know at the time that I made that commitment. When I told them about it, they advised me to try it for two months to see how it went. Everything went well and I lived there alone for eighteen years. I did move within the building, however. First, I was living on the west side with a view of the medical buildings. I didn't really like that area, so I moved to the east side, where it was pretty noisy. After that, I moved to the south side, which I was very pleased with. I made the place mine with furniture and plants and my own interior decorating.

It was rare at this apartment building to see other people in the elevators; usually it was just me. I did meet a girl in the elevator on the rare occasion, however, and we started chatting with each other. She lived in the apartment above me and wanted me to see her plants. She had one in particular that she didn't know recognize and wanted to see if I could identify it.

I couldn't. I don't really know the different kinds of plants; it's my mother who has the green thumb in the family. I know how to take care of house plants, but sometimes it can be difficult for me to differentiate between a plant and a weed!

The girl has become one of my closest friends now, and I think it's neat story about how we met.

My job at the Glenrose changed after seven and a half years of working in the playroom. I was slowly getting mentally burned out. I knew I would miss the kids like crazy, but I had to make a change.

The change was a good one. I was moved to the stroke victim unit and worked there for another seven and a half years. I really enjoyed that, too. The patients here were older than the kids I had been working with.

Working with people recovering from a stroke was similar in many ways to the work I was doing with the kids, but it was less taxing on me personally. The patients here had a more difficult time dealing with their new lives, because they had lived a longer life being completely healthy and able to do everything. It was a massive change for them.

I would do tasks that were helpful to the nurses, such as cleaning up messes, putting towels in the washrooms, cleaning the storage room, and communicating with recreation therapists. I also played games and talked with patients.

The stroke patients would watch me work and ask how I managed to do the things I did with only one good hand. They wanted to do the things I could do. I was able to tell them my story and give them hope that they would one day be able to function well, too. I would give them advice to do everything the therapist wanted them to do for a speedy recovery, and that coping with the disability made everything easier in the long run.

It's in me to talk to a lot of people. I love making friends. Anyone who wants to know what I have, I tell them. I'm an open book. The patients commented on me sometimes, saying that I had a smile like they couldn't believe. I know that God puts that smile on my face to help people and to encourage them in their lives and situations. I know that they can do what God wants them to do; they have a huge purpose in life. It's not up to me to know what that is, but I have strength from God to help give people credit, courage, understanding, and hope. I hope that's what people see when they meet me.

I hope that through talking with the kids in the playroom and the stroke victims their minds were geared to trying everything they could to get better—and get out of the hospital. It is hard work.

Many fun people worked in the stroke unit. One neurologist in particular loved to tease me. When I walked the halls, he would playfully, gently, sidecheck me into the wall. It was all fun and games. There were a lot of really nice doctors there and they all had fun with their work in different ways.

After the stroke unit, I began working as a porter. I did this for eight and a half years. This was great for me because I was able to speak with a lot of people this way. I delivered medicines, among other things, to the stroke unit, head injury unit, kids unit, and to people recovering from knee replacements.

Marlene Dawn Melnychuk

I operated a trolley run for the pharmacy. I would do six runs everyday: three in the morning and three in the afternoon. It was great at first, but I began to get tired by walking so much, so my runs eventually were cut down to four per day.

The atmosphere at the Glenrose was professional and busy, but still fun. With all jobs, though, it's what you make of it. If you're a cheerful person, you enjoy your job, but if you go into it as a negative person, the job won't be that fun.

I had a blast working with some of the people at the Glenrose, in all units. They soon realized that I loved to have fun and also play small pranks on them.

The best way to inspire people is to help them achieve all the things they once considered impossible.
—Unknown

Fun Stories from the Glenrose Hospital

In the stroke unit, a wonderful lady named Rosy cleaned the whole unit. She and I got along well together and I thought it would be fun to play some tricks on her.

One time, while she was in a room, she left her cleaning cart unattended. I grabbed it and rolled it into one of the elevators. She came out, saw it was missing, and asked where it was.

"I don't know," I said innocently.

She kept asking around, trying to find it.

One of the nursing staff must have seen me put it in the elevator because when she was asked about it she said, "I think Marlene rolled it into the elevator."

That was the end of the prank. Judging by the look on her face, Rosy was not completely impressed with me; I think she might have been a little annoyed.

I should have learned my lesson, but I played another prank on that poor woman. I knew Rosy was a smoker and took her breaks outside a couple of times a day. I decided to fill a latex glove with water and put it in the freezer overnight. In the morning, I put the frozen hand in the pocket of her winter jacket with the fingers pointed up. When she put on her jacket, she reached into her pockets to pull out her gloves. When her fingers touched the frozen fingers, she let out a scream that could be heard a long ways away. You could hear her all through the third floor. The nurses began calling me "Trouble."

Sometimes funny things would just happen at the Glenrose, which made for good stories to share with those who hadn't been there at the time they happened. Because of my lack of coordination, things usually seemed to happen to me.

One time, I took out the dirty laundry. I threw the heavy load down the chute, but as I tossed it down, the string of the laundry bag caught my foot. I almost went down the chute with the dirty laundry; instead I just slipped backwards and landed on my behind with my leg in the air.

Another time, I fell and the whole nursing unit saw the result of it. I had been trying to get a box of diapers back onto a shelf in the storage room. I took all the diapers out, then replaced them where they were supposed to be, but I lost my balance and fell into one of the big cardboard boxes sitting on the floor. I tried to get on my side, so that I might be able to wiggle myself out of the situation, but my head was where my knees were and there was no way to get out of this all by myself. I had to resort to yelling for help!

The nurses on the floor came running. Instead of helping me right away, like I was hoping for, they began to laugh. One of the nurses put a bow on my head while another one took pictures of me. It was pretty funny.

While working in the stroke unit, I might have made a mistake, but I'm not completely sure and I don't think I'll ever know. Some of the stroke patients in the unit had false teeth. The nurses would dress them in the morning and take them down to the cafeteria. On one of these days, one of the nurses forgot a patient's false teeth back in their room. I went to the room and saw the teeth—they were in a cup and they were dirty. I was freaked out about touching them, but I did it. I rinsed them out and might have put them in the wrong cup. I brought them downstairs. I couldn't remember who needed them, so I just guessed and gave them to someone there. I hope I got the right person, but to this day I'm still not sure.

In total, I worked at the Glenrose Rehabilitation Centre for twenty-four years. As acknowledgement, the staff gave everyone who had worked for twenty or more years a beautiful ring with the Glenrose symbol engraved on it. I have a gold ring with the old Glenrose flower symbol on it, and I love it. It's always on my finger.

Marlene Dawn Melnychuk

> *It is remarkable how many things people think they can't do when they are disabled.*
>
> *Do not be afraid to do the things you would like to do, because God will be with you in whatever you are doing.*
> —Unknown

ten

Travel Stories

I have had some exciting opportunities to see some of the other countries and places of the world. I love to travel and see God's creation. Even with my disability it is possible for me to do most of what I want to do.

I want people with disabilities to know that if you can do it, don't miss out on traveling. You should see as much as you can. There's a lot of beauty out there. Discover it for yourself.

Las Vegas

When I was eight years old, I saw Las Vegas for the first time. I remember falling asleep in the back our family's station wagon during the drive, and when I woke up I was greeted by lights—a lot of lights. These lights were blinking, swirling, and shaking. I'd never seen so many different kinds of lights on one street. It was night time, but the city made it seem like we were driving through during the day. I was entranced by the material beauty of it all.

The point of our trip wasn't to stay in Las Vegas, however. We were on our way to visit family in California.

California

We visited California many times while Wendi and I were growing up, but when I got older I began to go there by myself, or without my immediate family. We went to visit my aunt. She lived in a mobile home, so when we visited it was pretty crowded, but no one cared very much. The living room would be filled with bedding whenever she had guests.

The first time I went by myself was after I graduated from Grade Twelve. I travelled there just to visit my aunt and cousins; I was so thrilled to go on a plane by myself. Mom and Dad were a little bit nervous, but everything worked out great. It was easy; my parents dropped me off at one airport and my aunt picked me up at the other.

I stayed, of course, at my aunt's house. It was a beautiful holiday and we went to Disneyland and Knots Berry Farm. I went on a lot of rides at Disneyland with my cousins and had a blast.

I went again later with one of my cousins, Loretta. We wanted to go to Disneyland, but this time my aunt and cousins weren't with us.

"Marlene, do you know how to get to Disneyland?" Loretta asked.

"Yup," I said. "Of course I do. I've been there a couple of times."

Well, I think I would have known how to get there by car, but we took the bus and I had to admit that I really didn't know the way. We ended up asking the bus drivers a lot of questions. We made it there with hardly a problem and immediately started on the rides.

I was older now and Disneyland had a ride called Space Mountain. It looked so cool, so we eagerly took our spots in line. While we were in line, a couple of signs along the way cautioned against pregnant women, people with medical issues, and people with disabilities.

My cousin looked at me and asked, "Are you sure you want to go on this ride?"

There was no question in my mind—I was going to take on Space Mountain, whether or not the park thought it was a good idea. And I'm so glad that I did it. What a thrill!

Japan

I became a globetrotter when a girlfriend of mine asked me if I wanted to go to Japan with her. Joyce had friends there who were teaching English to Japanese children. I was almost at the end of working at the Glenrose Rehabilitation Centre at the time and had some banked holiday time, so before we knew it we were off flying across the world. We first had to fly to California to get the connecting flight to Japan. We were the only Caucasian people on the plane, and for some reason I immediately got a bit homesick.

Joyce's friends didn't meet us at the airport, so we had to find a way to get to them. We ended up waiting for a shuttle bus to take us to the train.

While we were waiting, a Japanese man came up to us and asked where we were trying to go. When we told him, he told us that we were in the wrong place; we had to go to another area to catch the bus. Then, to our surprise, he grabbed our bags and ran off in a different direction.

We didn't know if he was helping us or trying to steal our luggage. Whatever he was doing, we had to run after him to keep up. It felt like we were running for fifteen minutes before he finally stopped and showed us which bus to get onto. I was huffing and puffing after that—what a workout! I was glad he helped us, though, and that we had our suitcases with us once again.

Joyce's friend picked us up at the train station. It was a long trip, but we were happy to see Japan. When we walked into Joyce's friend's apartment, I couldn't believe how tiny it was. The place was barely bigger than a closet!

We rested up that evening and the next day we were invited to a Japanese woman's house for dinner. When we arrived, she lay out some kimonos for us to wear. I had a black and white one with flowers on it and, I must admit, it looked stunning on me. To get into the kimono, I had to suck in my stomach. That was hard to do; it didn't suck in so well. I couldn't breathe as well with the kimono on and I had to shuffle around when I walked.

She made all kinds of dishes that I had previously been oblivious to, living in Canada. One dish, I remember, was called "gold soup." The whole meal was so very good. I couldn't believe that I'd been missing out on this food my whole life.

Later, I saw a similar kimono in a store and it was pretty expensive. I think that it might be worth the price, though, since they are so beautiful.

We hadn't been in Japan for very long when we realized that the Japanese are very intrigued by blond-haired people. I had brown hair, so I didn't get too much attention, but Joyce had nice blond hair and they liked her very much.

We did some shopping and saw some of the sights. We went to some temples, too; they were impressive and each one had its own style. Some of them were plated with gold and others weren't. They were all beautiful.

We also visited a park where we met a lot of children. We had brought along with us a lot of Canadian buttons, which we handed out to the kids. They followed us around the park, curious about us.

In the park were magnificent cherry trees. They were in bloom at the time and were a sight to behold. The blossoms were falling to the ground. When you walked through the park, it was like walking through pink fluffy snow

I noticed that all the public places in Japan were kept clean. There weren't many dirty places there—at least, not that we saw.

A simple but wonderful memory I have of Japan is taking a bath back at the apartment. Joyce's girlfriend had a deep bathtub. When I filled it up, it just about covered my head; it was the most incredible bath. It was like sitting in a big pool, which was great because my feet were so sore from walking all over the place. I took my grand old time soaking in that bathtub.

One of the English as a Second Language (ESL) students drove us all over the country to see everything. We went shopping and I bought a sweater that I still really like; it wasn't very expensive.

To get around the country, we also took the bullet train. I had seen it once before on the trip, but this time we boarded it and it took us from place to place. There were three of us on the train and it was such a cool experience. I couldn't believe how fast we were actually going, but when I looked out the window it looked as though we were slowly going by everything. I knew that was an illusion—we were flying.

We stayed in Japan for two weeks in total and spent every night sleeping on a mattress on the floor of that small apartment.

I couldn't have asked for a better time! We had so much fun with each other.

After saying our goodbyes, Joyce and I went to the airport. We had to run to catch our plane. I enjoyed the flight a lot; it was an Australian airline, so a lot of the passengers and attendants had Australian accents. I think the Australian accent is my favourite accent.

We made a stop in Hawaii, wanting to visit there before returning home. I had been to Hawaii before, but I loved that I had an opportunity to go again. It is a stunning place to vacation and a perfect pace for me. It's not too busy, but it's also not boring.

Hawaii

We stayed in Hawaii for a couple of days, but I slept for ten hours that first night and day. Joyce went to the pool while I slept. I really needed the Hawaiian air to help calm down before I went back to work at the Glenrose. Joyce couldn't believe how long I slept, since I was usually up at 5:00 every morning.

When I had caught up on my sleep, we went to Honolulu. There was a pig roast taking place and it smelled so good. The entertainment was captivating and the food was amazing. It felt wonderful to be outside, well-rested, and well-fed.

We saw many of the sights in Hawaii and a lot of sun tanning on the island's beautiful beaches.

We made to fly to Maui and take in the sights there as well. We stayed in a condominium there, and nearby was a place where I was able to get some information on parasailing for handicapped people. I had seen people do it, and it really interested me.

Joyce didn't want to go parasailing, but she did go in the boat with me. I was really looking forward to flying.

They strapped me into a harness in a sitting position. One of the instructors threw out the parachute and then the driver gunned the boat. The parachute caught the wind, inflated, and they reeled me out into the clear blue sky. Flying high up in the heavens was one of the best feelings in the world. I felt so free.

I was so excited that my left arm started swinging back and forth with spasms. I could hear the instructors say, "Look at this girl! She's flying with one arm!"

I parasailed for about half an hour and took everything in, all the beauty of the ocean, sky, and the island. The beauty of God's creation was breathtaking. Everything was blue and green and wonderful. I spoke to every bird that flew by. What an amazing experience!

When they slowly pulled me back into the boat and I got closer to the ocean, I could see all kinds of colourful fish swimming happily below me. It occurred to me that there could be dolphins and whales down there, too, but I tried not to think about getting knocked over by a jumping whale.

They lowered me into the water, then pulled me into the boat again. Joyce said it had looked like a lot of fun and she thought she might try it herself someday.

As I mentioned, this was the second time I had visited Hawaii. The first time I was with my younger twin cousins Loretta and Lana and their girlfriends. They had just graduated from high school and going to Hawaii had been something they wanted to do before moving on to their careers. They invited me to go with them and I couldn't pass up the opportunity.

We went to many beaches and did a lot of tanning. I loved being in this paradise with such fun cousins. One night, we went out for supper while touring one of the islands. When we were done our meal, we still had room for dessert, so each of us ordered an ice cream treat.

Because of the tremors I get on my left side, I decided to sit on the edge of our booth, making it less likely for me to accidentally hit someone. I thought it was a good idea until I totally lost control of my arm.

We had ordered our desserts and the server came back with everyone's except for mine. She said that they didn't have what I wanted; I was disappointed but thought I should order something else. When I tried to get up, my arm went flying and made contact with the tray of ice cream desserts in our server's hand. The whole tray flew and all the treats crashed to the floor. There was no saving them; they were history.

The girls had quite the laugh at the whole incident. I felt a little embarrassed and sorry that I had hit the server, but I couldn't help laughing about it, too.

Hawaii was such a pleasure for me—both times. I enjoyed the company and feel blessed that I had more than one chance to vacation there.

Brazil

A while after the trip to Hawaii and Japan, my cousin Loretta wanted to go to Brazil. We had heard that it was beautiful there and it seemed like a fun place to visit. We found an affordable way to travel, but we knew that our method wasn't one that our parents would be happy about, so we led them to believe that we were going on a tour with other Canadians and Americans. The truth was that we were going on our own.

We were able to keep them believing this right up until the time we were leaving. It slipped out when my cousins and aunts were all at a baby shower together for another cousin. My mom overheard us talking about it and realized that we weren't actually going on a tour.

"You're not going, Marlene," she said. "It's not safe if you're not on a tour."

I just told her not to worry and that we would be fine.

We left two days after the baby shower.

My cousin and I flew into Rio de Janeiro and spent our first moments resting up at our hotel after a long flight. We were pretty jetlagged because of the flights and waiting times.

Our flight included a stopover in Toronto, where we had to wait seven hours before getting on our connecting flight. It was tiring but still fun. I don't mind airports too much because I'm a people watcher and Loretta was getting into it with me. We had a lot of fun talking amongst ourselves and watching all the different kinds of people walk by. Everyone was so interesting.

For the connecting flight itself, we got to sit in first class, which surprised me. It was so luxurious! We were given real silverware with our meal, not plastic forks and knives. They even had china to eat off of and glasses for our drinks.

I was seated in the aisle seat and, after being in the air awhile, I began to doze off. We hit some turbulence and I just about fell on the floor. It was a great flight.

We flew into Rio de Janeiro, went through customs, and right away found our hotel. We were so tired.

We were happy to meet a Canadian couple staying at the same hotel as us. Before we had left home. we had promised to phone our parents and tell them that we had arrived safely in Brazil. The problem was that we had to have some knowledge of Portuguese in order to be able to get access to the hotel's phone. The Canadian couple did speak Portuguese and helped us to figure out the phone so we could give our parents some peace of mind that we were okay. We got along with this couple and spent some time with them throughout our vacation.

Loretta and I spent our first two weeks touring around the city and enjoying some of the sights it had to offer.

We went shopping, but we had to take a taxi to get where we wanted to go. I took the front seat and off we went. It was a crazy drive and I held my hand over my eyes the whole way while the driver gabbed away, weaving in and out of traffic. With this man behind the wheel, what should have been a thirty-minute drive took half the time. I shakily got out of the taxi, happy to have my feet on steady ground again.

We found some great stores, and the prices were decent. The stores all had an "after Mardi Gras" sale and we ended up getting some nice souvenirs.

The next day, we toured a diamond and gem business. The diamonds and gems were brought to the business where they were made into all kinds of neat pieces. I saw a coffee table with flowers made out of gems. It was beautiful. Rubies were used for the petals of the roses; some roses were open and others weren't. The leaves were made out of other gems. It was gold-plated and very expensive. I found some more affordable items, too, and bought some jewellery. I couldn't help but get something; I wanted to always remember that place.

Even though I don't really like the colour of my birthstone, which is a light green for the month of August, I went ahead and bought a ring with my birthstone imbedded in it.

Obviously, we went to the beach, too. You can't go to Brazil and not go to a beach. So, the day after our shopping trip, Loretta and I caught a tour bus to downtown Rio de Janeiro. We got off close to the beach, crossed the street, and made our way toward the water. For me, it was like walking across a football field.

I was glad we went to the beach in the morning, because the sand wasn't so hot yet. It was just nice and warm. We found a nice spot on the beach and set ourselves up for relaxation. Lying in the sun and listening to the crashing of waves against the shore is one of the most serene environments to be a part of. We were both so tanned by the end of our holiday.

We made sure to take turns going swimming so that there was always someone watching over our purses and other possessions.

While we were at the beach, I was caught off guard by a local man with a cooler full of beverages. This man looked like me—not his face or anything, but he didn't have function in his left leg and arm, just like me. He looked like he had what I had. This man really touched my heart because in a way I could relate to him on a deep level, but in another way he seemed to be financially worse off than I was.

He was selling pop on the beach to try and make a living for himself, whereas I had been lucky enough to work at the Glenrose Rehabilitation Centre for a long time. I could afford to go on a holiday and enjoy a vacation, and he was probably just making enough to live.

It made me feel awful, but at the same time I thanked God that I'd had these opportunities. It really opened my eyes, because before this I hadn't thought too much about people who don't have anything to call their own. It was very humbling.

I hope that I can encourage other people to help those who need it and to care for others with different struggles.

That day at the beach was scorching hot, especially when morning turned into afternoon. Loretta and I decided to get off the scalding sand and back to our hotel. Even though Loretta was wearing flip-flops, the sand blistered her feet. I was wearing sandals. What was already a long walk seemed even longer.

As we were walking back to the hotel after dinner, we passed a group of five or six guys. Seeing that one was looking at me,

I got excited. My left arm started flying up and down and I scraped it on a rough wall as a result. When we got to our hotel, people asked me if I had been attacked on the walk back from the beach. I had to tell them the embarrassing story and was bandaged up by the staff at our hotel.

On our trip, Loretta and I decided it would be an adventure to go on a catamaran and travel around that way. It looked like the ship from *Gilligan's Island*. There were only seven passengers aboard and I felt like we were Mary Ann and Ginger. We travelled to some beautiful, white sandy beaches and had clean and comfortable places to stay.

That catamaran trip lasted for five days and four nights. On the last night, the crew caught some squid from the ocean. They served it to us, freshly caught. It was my first time eating squid; it was like chewing gum!

We met a guy from Rio de Janeiro on our catamaran trip who seemed to like both my cousin and me. When we docked in the city, as we were about to get off the catamaran, he kissed me and said, "Bye, girls."

He wanted to keep in touch and reunite sometime, but that hasn't happened. Maybe I should look him up?

When we sailed back port, just a little ways from Rio de Janeiro, we stayed at a different hotel. This hotel was more like a resort, and it was located on the beach. The staff here really liked Canadians and we were treated like royalty. We had a television in our room and the beds were on pedestals!

The way to the beach was interesting, too. There was a steep grade going down to the beach, so the resort had gondolas for their customers to travel down to the water.

Breakfast at the hotel was amazing. When we went to the restaurant, it was like we were two queens from Canada. We received such great service.

From this hotel we thought it would be a good idea to phone our parents and let them know when we were coming home.

We only stayed here for a weekend, but it was such a treat to have been at this resort.

Of all the days we stayed in Brazil, neither of us got sick from the food or anything else, and we only had one day of rain. The rain was incredible; we saw it coming in from the ocean and it looked like a tidal wave.

On the day we left, I got a stamp in my passport, said goodbye to Rio de Janeiro, and flew off into the sky. We landed in Toronto several hours later, and this time we only had to wait three hours before our connecting flight to Edmonton.

It was nice to go home after such a wonderful trip and tell family and friends about all the experiences we'd had.

Kelowna

I got a phone call from my cousin Lonnie, who invited me to visit his family in Kelowna, British Columbia, and help him landscape the front yard of his home. I thought this would be a really great time for a trip, so I said I would come in September.

I booked a flight. Mom and Dad dropped me off at the airport, and Lonnie picked me up when I arrived. We had a lot of fun remembering past memories.

When we got to their home, it was nice to see everyone. I got in and put my suitcase in order. Soon it was time for super.

In the evening, I had fun with their two children, but after a little while they were going to bed. Afterward, Lonnie and Lorrie discussed their landscaping project with me and how they wanted it done. When Saturday rolled around, we had a lot to do, but at the end of the day we finished everything. Boy, was I tried! But I got over it.

The next day, we all got up for church, and afterward I took them all out for dinner. When we got back, I thought we should take some pictures, so we did. That evening, we all that a relaxing time together.

Lonnie had to go to work on Monday, so I went shopping with Lorrie and the kids. When we got back, Lorrie's oldest girl wanted to go to her friend's house, so they went and I sat with their little guy. He watched as I took off my brace, then asked if he could try it on. "Why not?" I said. I helped him put it on. He really seemed to enjoy having it on and sat on the couch. When everyone got home, he asked his mom and dad if he could get one, and they said, "Talk to Auntie Marlene about that." That's when I told him why I had to wear it. He told me that he'd had a lot of fun putting it on.

The next day, I had to go home. Lonnie drove me back to the airport. I prayed in my heart that this time I had spent with my very special causing Lonnie and his family had been in God's hands. It was a somewhat relaxing time with people who are really special to me.

Cruise

With Catholic Social Services (CSS), I was happy to learn that I had the chance to go on a cruise with other clients of CSS, as well as support workers—including my support worker, Doreen. We flew to Vancouver, boarded the cruise ship, and headed to California.

This was my first time being on a cruise and I was surprised that I didn't have much trouble manoeuvring around the ship. My left leg seemed to take the slight movements well.

We made a stop in the city of Seattle's waterfront, where there was a big fishing area. They toured us around the city by bus and I could see that on almost every block there was either a Starbucks or a Second Cup. Even with all these coffee shops around, we didn't stop to taste what they had to offer. We went to a marketplace and shopped around while enjoying the sights. Then it was back onto the ship.

I don't remember exactly where we made the next stop, but I know that it was another fishing area. We saw how the people there cleaned the fish; it was like we were in a sardine shop. I also recall there being many ice cream shops there.

On the way home, we missed our connecting flight to Edmonton, so we had to travel on a small plane from Calgary to Edmonton. We had to exit the airport and go outside to board the plane. Doreen pushed me in a wheelchair toward the plane and I saw that the propellers were on the outside of the plane. You can't see that if you board by an enclosed ramp. I thought this was neat and pointed them out to Doreen. As I pointed, I saw the pilot wave at me. I think he thought I was waving at him, so he was waving back. He was pretty cute, so that was okay.

When we got inside the plane, he jokingly asked me if I wanted to sit up in the front with him. I didn't.

The whole trip was okay, but the difficult part was going with a lot of people I didn't really know. I also didn't know the woman I was bunking with for the trip. It was a challenge to make good friends in that short amount of time.

I think I would go on a cruise again, though, if I had another chance, but I would do it with friends or family. The ship itself is full of things to do and it's an easy way to see places.

Ontario

My most recent trip was to southern Ontario. My nephew Taryn and his bride were married in Mississauga in the summer. I went with my parents and we made a vacation out of it. The weather was warm and humid, which took some adjustment since we were coming from a drier and cooler climate.

Mom and Dad took me to Niagara Falls. When I saw the falls, I couldn't believe how magnificent they were. I had seen pictures of them, sure, but when I actually stepped up to the guardrail and looked over, words can't describe how powerful those waterfalls were. I was in awe. I was in even deeper awe when we boarded the great Maid of the Mist, a passenger boat that takes tourists right up to the falls. We could see the falls from the water level. The noise and mist all around us was incredible.

Before you board the boat, the company gives you blue plastic ponchos to wear. They look funny, but when you're at the bottom of Niagara Falls, with water spraying all around, you're glad to be wearing it.

Back at the top, at street level, are all kinds of attractions. There are so many shops with numerous souvenirs, haunted houses, a Ripley's Believe It Or Not museum, a Hershey's store, coffee shops, restaurants, and more. The streets in Niagara Falls are full of entertaining things to do and see.

If you look over the falls to the American side, already you can tell that Canada has a lot more to offer, visually. Maybe it's too far away to see what the American side actually looks like, but I can't imagine that they have the landscaping and gardens that the Canadian side has. Half the beauty of Niagara Falls is the many beautiful flowers that are in bloom. The American side looks bare and there aren't many people over on that side.

We came to Niagara Falls at a perfect time. The weather was great, everyone was happy, and we were treated to some daredevil entertainment—a man walking on tightrope strung over Niagara Falls. All he had up there with him was a pole to help him keep his balance. He must have been about thirties stories high and I heard some people around me saying that he was eighty years of age.

This daredevil walked the tightrope twice a day; once at four o'clock in the afternoon and then again at eight o'clock in the evening. We learned that he had started learning how to tightrope walk when he was just eighteen years old. I wish I could do that.

The special thing about him was that he donated everything he made to charities. I really liked this man.

I would definitely go back to Ontario. There's so much to see there and I'd like to experience more of what the province has to offer.

> So do not throw away this confident trust in the Lord. Remember the great reward it brings you! Patient endurance is what you need now, so that you will continue to do God's will. Then you will receive all that he has promised.
>
> "For in just a little while,
> the Coming One will come and not delay.
> And my righteous ones will live by faith..."
> —Hebrews 10:35–38 (NLT)

eleven

Brain Injury, Setbacks, and Stress Leave

During my last days at the Glenrose, I had a manager who I felt was adamant in getting rid of me. He caused me a lot of anxiety and eventually I had to leave the Glenrose on stress leave. A lot of people at the Glenrose were upset with him for pushing me out the door. They were saying things like, "That was a terrible thing for you to do, to throw Marlene out." Everyone supported me. It was hard to deal with. I thought it would be nice to keep working and have some extra money, but if my health isn't there, then what would be the point? The stress from the manager wasn't worth risking my health, so off I went. I was done in 2003.

I went to live with my parents again. At this time, they were living in Sherwood Park. It was here that I had a bad fall. I was at my parents' place and they had left for the day. My computer was downstairs and I went upstairs to get a bowl of white cherries. When I came back downstairs, I lost my balance and fell down the stairway. The bowl of cherries went flying.

I don't remember too much, but I was later told everything that happened. I had gone headfirst down the flight of stairs and was unconscious when I hit the bottom. I lay there for about three hours until my mom found me. She called the ambulance in a panic. She had tried to ask me what had happened, but I didn't respond. She knew I had been severely injured.

I began to regain consciousness as the ambulance arrived. I'm told that I was very irritated as they were taking care of me. They put a neck brace on me and I tried to fight them. I didn't want it on me. They had to tie me down when I tried to rip out the IV they'd given me.

I was put in the intensive care unit at the Royal Alexander Hospital to recover. The doctors were concerned about me having a brain haemorrhage and monitored me for five days. I had a severe head injury.

During these five days, the doctors realized that I had lost my short-term memory and sense of smell. I was also hallucinating; sometimes it was so bad that they would have to strap me to the bed during the night to keep me from physically fighting whatever it was I wanted to fight. They would loosen the straps during the day.

There were a few other patients in the ICU with me, and one morning the nurses told my parents that I had been singing almost nonstop the whole night. When they asked me to be quiet for the other patients I just said, "What can I do?" and kept singing.

After the five days, I began to calm down and recovered at a good pace. I spent five weeks at the Royal Alexandra Hospital and three weeks at the Glenrose Rehabilitation Centre.

The first three weeks at the Royal Alex weren't look so good. The prognosis was very bad. I had a cracked skull, swelling in the brain, and had to worry about having surgery and coming out of it. The doctors said that I would have a lot of scars from the surgery.

I was very fortunate. My parents had just started a sabbatical at the time of the accident and were home most days. If this had happened a couple of days earlier, it could have been too late for me by the time someone got home.

My parents and my sister were close to me during this time. They prayed for me and spent many hours by my bedside while I was recovering. I know that this was a shock to them, too, and it had really heightened their fears of me falling again.

After I spent my time at the Glenrose, in rehab, I still had to go back for two more years for therapy. I had many sessions with the psychologist there.

Mom and Dad left me at home for a couple of hours one day, and I thought I would do a little Bible study. The radio was on and I heard Michael W. Smith's song, "Healing Rain." As I listened to it, I started to cry on account of the blessing God had put in my heart.

I also went to Grant MacEwan University and took a course after I fell. I was part of the People with Physical Disabilities organization, which was able to help me get into this class. It was a communications course in which we practiced our speaking skills. It was a five-day course and I two years in a row; the class really helped train my mind to speak well. My brain was getting better at language skills and I did get my diploma. I also spoke at my graduation.

I almost made a complete recovery and am so thankful that things weren't worse than what they could have been. I'm pretty sure that everything came back to me. I'm not completely sure, but I feel like I'm back to normal. It is a miracle that I recovered so well.

Never give up on the things you really want to do. The person with the biggest dreams is more powerful than the one with all the facts.
—Unknown

twelve

Life After Brain Injury

I think each of us is chosen by God for certain things. We don't always know what those things are, but I believe the bad things we go through are always for a greater purpose. So many times when you face unknown or difficult times, you say, "Why me? Why this?" But through questioning God, I've learned to trust Him, and through that I have gained so much strength knowing that He is in control.

Catholic Social Services

Before I fell, and after I finished working at the Glenrose, I applied to Catholic Social Services. The Glenrose had put in a request for me at CSS, and soon after my fall I was paired up with my support worker, Doreen.

Doreen and I meet once a week. She checks to see how things are going in my life and we go grocery shopping together. Getting groceries with Doreen is really helpful, since she pushes the cart down the aisles for me so I can concentrate on what I need to buy for that week.

Doreen has been a great match for me. She helps me with what I need, but she doesn't hover over me all the time and only helps me when I want her to. I know it's hard for her to watch if I fall when she's her, but I'm really glad that she doesn't treat me like I can't do anything. She treats me really well.

Catholic Social Services is an organization that strives to help people of all faiths and backgrounds live with a sense of purpose and dignity. CSS has many programs for young mothers, new immigrants, families, persons with disabilities, among others. Their mission is to enhance the lives of people who need it and to carry out this goal with sensitivity and compassion. CSS has a number of staff and many volunteers to help them be successful.

I am very grateful for CSS. I like being a part of their group and they have helped enhance my life, making it easier for me to live independently.

Working on This Book

When I was about eighteen years old, God spoke to me. He told me to write down the story of my life. I was confused. I didn't think that I had a story. Nothing I could think of would be interesting to people, or so I thought, but He convinced me to write this book. With the help of CSS and its volunteers, I have finally been able to do it.

I have been working on this book for a while, trying to come up with all the stories I could remember and their details. It's been a long time coming, but the book is finally finished and I'm so happy to share my story with anyone who wants to read it.

Independent Living Near Whyte Avenue

After my fall, I lived with another girl who had a disability. I didn't know her before we moved in together. Living with her was really difficult; my patience didn't go very far. It seemed like she never wanted to talk with me.

I feel like there were some weird things going on. Her parents were a little odd as well. It seemed like she had everyone wrapped around her baby finger. Rent was also fairly expensive for me. It wasn't very pleasant living there and I was looking for another place.

Doreen and I looked around and heard about an apartment close to Whyte Avenue that was available for rent. Doreen and I rushed over and I was able to rent the apartment. I'm still here and I really like it. It's nearby to shopping and not too far away from the services I need.

I have an amazing next door neighbour. She lived through World War II and has some amazing stories to tell. She'll visit with me sometimes and bring over delicious baked goods. I really value her as a neighbour and friend. I hope that we're neighbours for a long time.

I can often be seen jetting around parts of the city with Sky Dawn, the electric scooter that I've had since 2005. It's red and easy to handle. Because my left arm sometimes has spasms, the scooter helps. I can pin my arm between my side and the arm rest so that it doesn't get out of control. The scooter is also great for traveling longer distances so that I don't have to tire myself out by walking.

I got it brand new and the brand name was Cobra. I wanted to name it something more ladylike, so I came up with Sky

Dawn. I love the name: Dawn is my middle name and I chose the name Sky just because I love looking at the sky. It's always beautiful and always changing.

If I do need to go further away for something, I take the Disabled Adult Transit System (DATS) bus to get there. It costs the same as public bus services and I can get a monthly pass. They pick me up right at my door; it's so convenient for me. I have to call for it a couple of days ahead of time, but it's a really great service to have in the city.

My Family

My family has been so supportive and helpful with my work to get back on my feet. I feel so much love from them and am really grateful that they are around to visit and help me if and when I need it.

My family grew used to watching me all the time and making sure I didn't trip or fall. I understand that they love me too much to have anything happen to me, but sometimes I feel like I'm in a closed umbrella with people all around me telling me how to do things. My love of independence sometimes clashes with their protective ways. I love to be independent, and sometimes it's difficult when they show their love for me in that way. However, I do know that if anything were to happen again they would be right by my side through it all—no matter what.

In General

I want to have a full life. As much as I can do, I want to do. There is always something that can spark my interest. I love maintaining a social life and doing everyday activities. On the weekends, I like to go out with girlfriends and see movies or plays, or just go for coffee and chat. I have some really great friends.

One of my friends really touched my heart after she gave birth to a beautiful baby girl. The baby, who is now a charming young girl, was born prematurely with Down's syndrome and, as a newborn in the hospital, had tubes coming out of her body. My friend told me that she named her little daughter with the middle name Dawn, after me. She wanted to have a little bit of me in her daughter. I couldn't believe it! I felt so honoured.

When I visited them in the hospital, my friend had to run to the washroom, so she gave her daughter to me to hold. She put her on a soft pillow and placed her on my lap. I held her and sang to her—it felt so good to hold such a beautiful newborn baby. That was a wonderful gift my friend gave to me.

Sometimes I go to public recreation facilities to do exercises or go in the pool; I like to see what I can do to better myself. I go to banquets and galas for different events and I love meeting new people and enjoying the food and dances.

I can prepare meals for myself. I'm too nervous to share my cooking with other people, though, even though I eat my own cooking. My favourite thing to eat is spareribs with barbecue sauce. I like to make pasta dishes and soup. I also do my own laundry.

I phone my mom and dad all the time. I think I phone them once a day, and sometimes it's twice a day. They come and visit me at my apartment just to talk and to see how I'm doing.

If I find I have an afternoon or evening free, I'll play games on the computer, e-mail, read books, or watch television or a movie. If I have people over, I love to play board games.

World Vision Sponsor

I surprised my mother and father one day when I told them they had a new granddaughter. I explained to them that I had sponsored a little girl from Haiti who was four years old.

I love being a sponsor. I used to get letters from this girl and give letters and small gifts to her as well. When she turned eighteen, I could no longer sponsor her, which broke my heart. Today, I sponsor a little boy from Haiti. It's nice to have these connections and know that I can make a difference in their lives.

Toastmasters

I first heard about Toastmasters on 105.9 SHINE FM in Edmonton. They promoted it as a fun group that learned the skills of public speaking. I kept hearing about it on the radio until I thought, *Why shouldn't I try it?* The Lord said, "Go for it, Marlene." So I did.

I liked it right away. It was a lot of fun and I got to meet a lot of other Christians. There were about twelve people who regularly went to Toastmaster group I was part of. The group met from 7:30 to 9:30 on Tuesday nights at King's University College. It was a great thing for me to do after my brain injury and helped me learn how to public speak. It was therapeutic as well, as it helped me practice my sentences and words. These Toastmaster exercises also helped me to think a little quicker.

I've been in Toastmasters for over three years now to maintain my speaking skills. I'm trying to do my best in the club and am the vice-president for public relations for our group. My job is to call around and talk with people, introducing them to the club. I've also had to get out posters for our meetings around the city.

If anyone is interested in joining Toastmasters, it's really easy. You can see if you like it first by just sitting in on one of the sessions. If you like it, come again.

One of the exercises involves sitting around a table in a group with a bell on the table. One person speaks about whatever they want to talk about and everyone else listens. If the person talking says "Ahh" or "Umm," someone else dings the bell. It's a great way to learn how to stop doing that during a speech.

I've learned from Toastmasters how to prepare a speech as well. You make a speech like a sandwich—with a beginning, middle, and end. It's encouraged to use visual aids to make your speech more engaging as well. I've learned so much and I really think it has helped me with day to day speaking as well as addressing groups of people.

Soon after I began Toastmasters, I was asked to speak to some Grade Eleven and Twelve students at the General Hospital in Edmonton. It was a kind of class for the ones who were thinking about going into the medical field when they graduated from high school. I had some confidence from being in Toastmasters, and I generally love to talk, so I was pretty excited to have the opportunity to tell my story to these young people.

For my first session, I spoke to about sixty kids. I had so much fun and enjoyed their questions. It was a thrill to be up there, teaching them about encephalitis from a personal perspective.

The hospital asked me back again and again and I was always happy to say yes. For the third and fourth years, I spoke to ninety young people at a time. I'm so overjoyed to have these opportunities. I tell my story and they are really absorbed by what I'm saying. I know that these words are put in my mind by God. He has helped me so much.

I have also been asked to deliver the children's message at the Ukrainian church on Thanksgiving Day. I'll tell my story to the children and show them how thankful to God I am for His providence throughout my life. I'm looking forward to this.

Marlene Dawn Melnychuk

One of the most interesting gifts we all possess is the ability to dream.

Our hearts have desires that bring our thoughts to those dreams, often throughout our life journey.

If you view your dreams as reality, it will only be a matter of time before you make them come true.

Note that your heart's desire is only a dream away.

—Unknown

thirteen

Future Goals and Dreams

I still have many goals. I'm not dead yet! I believe that there's more I can do and people I can help.

One of the top goals I have for myself is skydiving. After I went parasailing in Hawaii, I was hooked on that kind of adventure. A step higher is skydiving. I would like to go tandem; I don't trust myself to go alone. I'd rather be strapped to a professional skydiver. It would be a total rush to be that high in the air, then jump out of a plane, freefall, and float to the ground. I can't think of anything that would be more thrilling.

Another goal is getting this book published and being able to distribute it to all kinds of places. I hope this book will be read by many people. I want it to be an inspiration to people who have dealt with encephalitis or something similar, and I hope the book will shed light on encephalitis for people who don't understand what it is. I don't think there are many published books about people with encephalitis. I know that there are textbooks about it, but it's good to read about the perspective of someone who actually has it.

I would also like to speak publicly anywhere in the country about living with encephalitis and the things God has given me strength to do, even with a handicap. I really want to encourage people to discover the gifts God has given them and not to be discouraged by the difficulties they face.

When I know I'm going to share my story, either with this book or in daily life, I take a deep breath and pray, "Lord, please give me the words to say to these people who are hurting inside. Share my experiences with them and help me lift them up in their frame of mind to help them cope with their life struggles."

I also want to speak with medical doctors to get their understanding of my book and promote the person as well as the facts of the disease. I really am thankful to doctors and nurses and other medical workers; without their help and care, life for me today would be a lot different. I would like to talk with them and show them that they really make a positive difference in the lives of the people they work with.

Traveling is also on my list of goals. I love to travel and hope I am given the opportunity to do so again sometime in the near future.

I hope I can accomplish these things in my life—and more, if God lets me know what He needs me to do.

CPSIA information can be obtained at www.ICGtesting.com
Printed in the USA
LVOW051929050612

284799LV00004B/1/P